ProBASIC

Professional Modular BASIC Programming

Alan Bird

Produced by:
Brian Wiser & Bill Martens

 Apple PugetSound Program Library Exchange

ProBASIC: Professional Modular BASIC Programming

ACKNOWLEDGEMENTS

ProBASIC was programmed by Alan Bird and published by The Software Touch in 1985. We would like to thank Alan Bird for creating so many tools that were beneficial for Apple II users.

This new manual, produced in coordination with Alan Bird and released with his permission, is copyright by A.P.P.L.E.. No claim to copyright over *ProBASIC* is created outside of those portions created by A.P.P.L.E..

ProBASIC disk images are available from the A.P.P.L.E. website: www.callapple.org. No warranty of disk images is made or implied and should be used at your own risk.

PRODUCTION

Brian Wiser   →   Cover, Design, Layout, Editing, Proofreading
Bill Martens   →   Initial Manual, Software Updates, Production

DISCLAIMER

About the Author

Alan Bird

Alan Bird has been a software engineer for decades, encompassing the Apple II, Mac, iOS, and other platforms. In 1984 he accepted a position with Beagle Bros in San Diego, which was a very popular Apple II software company known for its signature ads and product documentation that featured old-time artwork. There he developed programming utilities like *Fatcat*, *D Code*, *Extra K*, and *Beagle Compiler*.

In 1986, Alan partnered with fellow Beagle developer Mark Simonsen to form a small software company called The Software Touch. They developed four products for that company along with *TimeOut* add-ons for the popular productivity program *AppleWorks*. Because of their experience with developing *AppleWorks* add-ons, Beagle Bros was hired by Apple to develop version 3 of *AppleWorks*.

In 1990, he joined with another Beagle Bros spinoff called WestCode Software. There he developed a couple of applications for the Apple IIGS and his first Macintosh application, *OneClick*.

In 1996, Alan started work for a rising star in the telecommunications industry, Qualcomm. He spent about five years as part of the Macintosh developer team creating *Eudora* – one of the earliest and most widely-used Internet email applications.

Read more about Alan and his computing history at: https://alanlbird.wordpress.com

About the Producers

Brian Wiser

Brian Wiser is a long-time consultant, enthusiast and historian of Apple, the Apple II and Macintosh. Steve Wozniak and Steve Jobs, as well as *Creative Computing*, *Nibble, InCider*, and *A+* magazines were early influences.

Brian designed, edited, and co-produced many books including: *Nibble Viewpoints: Business Insights From The Computing Revolution*, *Cyber Jack: The Adventures of Robert Clardy and Synergistic Software*, *Synergistic Software: The Early Games*, *The Colossal Computer Cartoon Book: Enhanced Edition*, *What's Where in the Apple: Enhanced Edition,* and *The WOZPAK: Special Edition* – an important Apple II historical book with Steve Wozniak's restored original, technical handwritten notes.

He passionately preserves and archives all facets of Apple's history, and noteworthy related companies such as Beagle Bros and Applied Engineering, featured on AppleArchives.com. His writing, interviews and books are featured on the technology news site CallApple.org and in *Call-A.P.P.L.E.* magazine that he co-produces. Brian also co-produced the retro iOS game *Structris*.

In 2005, Brian was cast as an extra in Joss Whedon's movie *Serenity*, leading him to being a producer and director for the documentary film *Done The Impossible: The Fans' Tale of Firefly & Serenity*. He brought some of the *Firefly* cast aboard his Browncoat Cruise and recruited several of the *Firefly* cast to appear in a film for charity. Brian speaks about his adventures to large audiences at conventions around the country.

Bill Martens

Bill Martens is a systems engineer specializing in office infrastructures and has been programming since 1976. The DEC PDP 11/40 with ASR-33 Teletypes and CRT's were his first computing platforms with his first forays in the Apple world coming with the Apple II computer.

Influences in Bill's computing life came from *Byte* magazine, *Creative Computing* magazine, and *Call-A.P.P.L.E.* magazine as well as his mentors Samuel Perkins, Don Williams, Joff Morgan, and Mike Christensen.

Bill is a co-producer of many books including *What's Where in the Apple: Enhanced Edition, The WOZPAK: Special Edition, Nibble Viewpoints: Business Insights From The Computing Revolution,* and co-programmer for the iOS version of the retro game *Structris.* He has written many articles which have appeared in user group newsletters and magazines such as *Call-A.P.P.L.E.*.

Bill worked for Apple Pugetsound Program Library Exchange (A.P.P.L.E.) under Val Golding and Dick Hubert as a data manager and programmer in the 1980s, and is the current president of the A.P.P.L.E. user group established in 1978. He reorganized A.P.P.L.E. and restarted *Call-A.P.P.L.E.* magazine in 2002. He is the production editor for the A.P.P.L.E. website CallApple.org, writes science fiction novels in his spare time, and is a retired semi-pro football player.

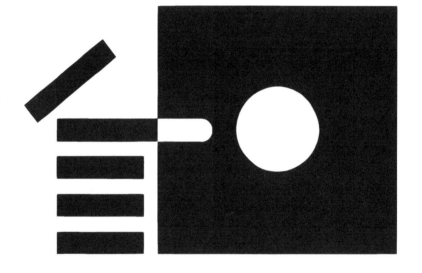

CONTENTS

Introduction to ProBASIC

Programming

System Modules

Changes to ProDOS

Library Modules

Additional Libraries

INTRODUCTION TO
PROBASIC

ProBASIC enhances the Applesoft BASIC that is built-in to your Apple II series computer. It allows you to add new commands and functions called modules to your programs. This capability is called "extensibility" because the language actually grows.

These modules may be written in either BASIC or machine language. Machine language modules may be written to greatly increase the speed of your programs. Those programmers not familiar with machine language can still easily use machine language modules written by other programmers. BASIC modules add modularity and structure that make it much easier to edit, debug and maintain your programs. Additionally, the modules may be saved on disk and easily integrated into other programs.

Proper use of *ProBASIC* modules will make your programs run faster and will make them much easier to understand for making changes. Variable conflicts are also much easier to avoid since each BASIC module has its own set of variables (local variables). Programs should be broken down into modules of not more than 30 or 40 lines that can be easily understood and quickly edited. Each module can be independently tested and re-used in other programs. Programmers familiar with structured languages such as Pascal and C will quickly see the similarities between a *ProBASIC* module and a procedure or function.

Installing *ProBASIC*

ProBASIC disk images can be downloaded from the publisher's site: www.callapple.org. Simply boot the *ProBASIC* disk to install *ProBASIC*. If you have already booted with another ProDOS disk, you may enter "-PRO.SYSTEM" to start *ProBASIC*.

This version of *ProBASIC* includes ProDOS 2.4.2 or later, which allows the included disk image to run on any Apple II computer as long as it has a minimum of 64K of memory. Older Apple II's including the Apple II and Apple II Plus will require the Language Card with an additional 16K of memory, while the IIe, IIc, and IIGS require no further hardware.

Using *ProBASIC*

After installing *ProBASIC* you will receive the Applesoft prompt ("]") and will be able to program as usual in BASIC except that you may additionally use the following system modules:

HELP – Lists all modules.

EDIT – Allows editing and/or lising of a BASIC module.

MAKE – Creates a BASIC module.

ELSE – For use in IF/THEN/ELSE statements.

PARM – Allows passing of parameters to a BASIC module.

EXIT – Returns from a module to whatever called it.

FLAG – Used to change the operation of certain *ProBASIC* functions.

and you will also have these additional ProDOS commands:

MODLOAD – Loads modules from disk into the language.

MODSAVE – Saves BASIC modules to disk.

There are also a few sample programs included that you may load and run and/or list to learn how to use modules. These programs have a file type of "PRG". Included with *ProBASIC* is a special version of the "Program Writer" editor that will work with *ProBASIC*, called "PRO.EDITOR". A new command has been added that allows you to switch to a different module. Use the a-h command and enter the name of the module you wish to edit or press <RETURN> to edit the main program.

PROGRAMMING

Using Modules

A program in *ProBASIC* consists of the main program and zero or more modules. The main program itself is a BASIC module called "MAIN". When you RUN a *ProBASIC* program, the main program (MAIN) is run. It may then call other modules.

Once a module has been created or loaded from disk, it is called just like a standard BASIC statement or function and for all practical purposes the module has become a part of the BASIC language just as much as FOR or NEXT or any of the others. All modules are both statements and functions. They may be executed without returning a value like the statements HGR or GOTO. Every module may also be called as a function that returns a value such as SIN or PEEK.

Modules may be called from the main program or from BASIC modules. Like BASIC commands, a module may require one or more parameters. Parameters are values that are passed to the statement or module. For example, the statement POKE 36,20 has 2 parameters: 36 and 20. The first parameter is an address and the second parameter is the value to poke into that address.

When typing a module name into a program, a space must follow the name if it is to be followed by any parameters. For example, TEST A,B,C is correct, TESTA,B,C is not. This is to help *ProBASIC* interpret the name of the module correctly. In the preceding example if there was a module call TESTA it would be impossible for *ProBASIC* to determine if TESTA was being called or TEST with a parameter A. That is why a module name must always be followed by a space if there are any parameters.

Another difference between BASIC and *ProBASIC* is that all parameters for a BASIC or machine language module may optionally by surrounded by square brackets ([ ]). For example, TEST in the preceding example may be called like this: TEST [A,B,C]. Sometimes

3

this is necessary to separate parameters. If, for example, BOX requires 3 parameters and TEST is one of the parameters, an expression such as BOX X,TEST A,B,C,Y is misleading because it appears that TEST has 4 parameters when actually Y should belong to BOX. The correct syntax for the expressions should be BOX X,TEST [A,B,C],Y.

Starting New Programs

Before starting a new program you need to determine if the program will be using either of the hi-res graphics pages. Use NEW by itself to create a new program or use it with one of the following parameters depending on which memory configuration you will require. For example, if you are not going to use any hi-res graphics, use the NEW TEXT command.

NEW TEXT   Prepares for a new program that will not use any hi-res graphics. The program will start at $2000 (8192). Using this command will give you 8K more programming space.

NEW [HGR]   Prepares for a new program that will use hi-res graphics page 1. The program will start at $4000 (16384). Using the HGR parameter is optional. Since HGR is the default parameter, typing only NEW is the same as NEW HGR.

NEW HGR2   Prepares for a new program that will use hi-res graphics page 2. The program will start at $6000 (24576). This will not leave you very much program space.

VERY IMPORTANT: If you are planning on using any hi-res graphics in the program you are writing, it is important to do the correct NEW command before you start on the program because you cannot change it later. An incorrect NEW command may cause graphics commands to wipe out your program!

Memory Map

The *ProBASIC* program resides at $0C00 (3072) to $1FFF (8191). The area from $0800 to $0BFF (2048 to 3071) is free and you may use it for text page 2 or lo-res graphics page 2 or for extra memory for your modules. The module VIRTUAL uses it for a 1K ProDOS buffer so do not use it if you are using VIRTUAL. Page 3 ($0300) is not used by *ProBASIC*. HIMEM has been lowered to make room for the new ProDOS commands MODLOAD and MODSAVE.

STOP AND CONT

If a STOP is entered in a module or a control-C is pressed while a module is executing, *ProBASIC* will stop with editing set up for the module the stop occurred in. To determine which module you stopped in, just press <RETURN> after the BASIC prompt (]). A CONT command will resume in the module that the program stopped in.

Handling Errors

The ONERR GOTO statement works normally except when a BASIC module is called. Refer to the following illustration in the explanation that follows where MODULE1 calls MODULE2 which calls MODULE3:

```
 -----------        -----------        -----------
| MODULE1 |  --> | MODULE2 |  --> | MODULE3 |
 -----------        -----------        -----------
```

If MODULE1 sets up an ONERR GOTO and calls MODULE2 which sets up its own ONERR GOTO and calls MODULE3 which does not set up an ONERR GOTO and has an error, MODULE3 will be exited immediately and processing will continue at the ONERR GOTO which MODULE2 has set up. If MODULE2 had not set up an ONERR GOTO and an error occurred in MODULE3, both modules would be exited immediately and the ONERR would be handled in MODULE1.

5

If none of the modules has set up an ONERR, the program will stop and print the error message. When an error occurs in a BASIC module, *ProBASIC* will stop with editing set up for the module that caused the error so you just press RETURN to determine which module caused the error or LIST it to determine what caused the problem.

SYSTEM MODULES

Overview

The following describes in detail how to use the system modules. System modules are no different from any other machine language *ProBASIC* module except that they are built-in.

Some system modules require parameters – expressions following the name of the system module that specify more specifically what you want the system module to do. After the name of each module will be a list of all the possible parameters. Optional parameters are enclosed in square brackets ("[ ]").

Numeric parameters are numeric expressions such as:

`25:`	Numeric constant
`N:`	Numeric variable
`2+A%*6:`	Numeric expression
`SIN (30):`	Function
`TEST 4:`	Module that returns a numeric value

String parameters are string expressions such as:

`"Hello":`	String constant
`S$:`	String variable
`A$+B$+C$:`	String expression
`MID$ (A$,2,3):`	Function
`TEST:`	Module that returns a string value

In the examples, don't enter the "]". <RETURN> means enter the RETURN key.

HELP [module number] – Lists all modules

Entering HELP will list the modules for the program that's in memory including system modules (see example below). The first column contains the module number. Entering the module number as a parameter for HELP will list the modules starting with the module with the specified module number. Every HELP thereafter will start with that module. This may be necessary if you have many modules and only want to see the last few that were added or if you don't want to always see the system modules listed. To start from the top of the list again, enter: HELP 1.

The next column contains the address of the module in memory. The address may be useful to machine language programmers who need to debug a machine language module or to the curious who are interested in seeing the structure of BASIC modules. If a module is disk-based (see DISK in library modules) the address will be replaced by the word DISK.

The next column contains either ASM for a machine language module or BAS for a BASIC module. When you first load in *ProBASIC*, there will not be any BASIC modules.

The final column is the name of the module. This is the name supplied when you MAKE a module or load it from disk (see MODLOAD in NEW DOS COMMANDS). Examples:

```
]HELP

0   $4001 BAS MAIN      ;the main program
1   $1341 ASM HELP      ;system modules
2   $1344 ASM EDIT
3   $1347 ASM MAKE
4   $134A ASM ELSE
5   $134D ASM PARM
6   $1350 ASM EXIT
7   $1353 ASM FLAG
8   $1FFF ASM SEARCH    ;user-added machine language module
9   $2080 BAS AVERAGE   ;user-added BASIC module
10  DISK BAS DOSUM      ;disk-based BASIC module

]HELP 7                 ;will start listing from 7th module
```

8

MAKE [module name] – Creates a BASIC module

Use MAKE to create a new BASIC module. The module name may be any length but a maximum of 8 characters is recommended. Longer names may lower the maximum number of modules you may have in your program. Any characters may be used in the module name but the 1st character must be alphabetic (A-Z). Any spaces will be removed. All characters in the module name are significant.

You may MAKE modules that replace standard BASIC commands and functions. For example, you may MAKE a DRAW module that will replace the Applesoft BASIC DRAW command.

After MAKEing the module you can type in program lines to define the module. To return to the main program or to edit/list another module, use EDIT.

Even while you are typing in the lines for module, you may call the module to test it. You do not need to return to the main program or to another module to call the module you are making. The maximum number of modules you may have including system modules is 255. Examples:

```
]MAKE CUBE

]MAKE PRINT.HEADING

]MAKE GET_INPUT
```

Possible Errors

KEYWORD TABLE FULL: Cannot add another module because there is no more room to store the name of the module. You should've used shorter module names. This will only occur if you have close to the maximum number of modules created and the average module name is over 8 characters.

EDIT [module name] – Specifies module to edit/list

After creating a module and typing in the program lines for the module, it is almost always necessary to go back and make changes. Use EDIT to specify which module you need to edit and/or list. The module name must be one that has already been created. To edit the main program (MAIN), enter EDIT with no module name.

If you forget which module you are editing, press <RETURN> and the name of the module will be listed in "/ /". If you are editing the main program, no module name is listed. Examples:

```
]EDIT DRAW.SQUARE      ;edit DRAW.SQUARE
]LIST                  ;list module

10 PARM S
     .
     .
     .
100 EXIT
```

EXIT [return value] – Returns from a module to whatever called it

Returns: the parameter is returned to the calling module.

Every BASIC module must end with an EXIT statement to return properly to whatever called it (the main program or another module). If the module does not end with an EXIT statement, the program will end as soon as the end of the module is reached just as if the end of the main program were reached or an END statement were executed.

A module may act as a function by specifying a return value. A function is something that returns one string or numeric value. Examples of built-in Applesoft functions are LEN, LEFT$, SIN, PEEK, and INT. These all return a value that may be assigned to a variable, printed, used as part of an expression, or even used as a parameter to another function.

In the same way, modules may return a value to whatever called it using the EXIT statement. If no return value is specified, a module will always return 0 if used as a function. Examples:

```
100  EXIT X        ;returns value of X

100  EXIT A * B / 2

100  IF A = B THEN EXIT "YES" ELSE EXIT "NO"

100  EXIT [A]

100  EXIT          ;just exits, returns 0
```

PARM variable [, variable] – Passes parameters to a BASIC module

Returns: Number of parameters passed.

When a module is called, it has its own set of variables and does not have access to the variables of whatever called it. For example, if a module "TEST" is called from the main program and the main program has a variable "I", the module "TEST" will not use the variable "I" from the main program but may create its own variable "I". This is known as having local variables.

The advantages of local variables are many. It means that a module will not accidently change the value of a variable from the main program or from another module. Often BASIC programmers will write a subroutine with FOR/NEXT loops that use the variable "I" or a counter "N". If these variables are also used by the program that called it, the subroutine may accidently change the values of the variables and they will have the wrong values when the subroutine returns. By using modules with local variables instead of subroutines, this will never happen. This also means that it is easy to write a module that may be transferred to another BASIC program, regardless of which variables the program uses.

Most modules will require some information from whatever called it. Since variables are local there must be some way of passing that data into the module.

For example, let's write a module that will print a certain character a certain number of times. Let's call the module REPEAT. We need to tell REPEAT which character to print and how many times to print it. To get that information into REPEAT, we use the PARM statement. We will define REPEAT like this:

```
MAKE REPEAT
10   PARM A$,N
20   IF N = 0 THEN 40: REM Don't print any
30   FOR I = 1 TO N: PRINT A$;: NEXT
40   PRINT : REM Print carriage return
50   EXIT
```

If we now call REPEAT with this, it will print 10 *'s.:

```
REPEAT "*",10
```

When REPEAT is entered, the variable A$ will receive the value "*" and N will receive 10. We could also call REPEAT with the following values:

```
REPEAT S$, X
REPEAT CHR$(7), N/2
REPEAT "Hello"+CHR$(13), PEEK (35)-1
REPEAT A$(I), A(I)
```

The type of parameter passed must be the same type as the variable that will receive it. If, for example, we do:

```
REPEAT 3," ---"
```

the result will be a TYPE MISMATCH error because the value 3 which is numeric cannot be passed to the variable A$ because it is a string variable and the string expression " ---" cannot be passed to the numeric variable N. You may, however, pass an integer value to a real variable or a real value to an integer variable. The following is valid even though X% is integer and it is being passed to N which is a real variable:

```
REPEAT "@",X%
```

A PARM statement can be used at any time in the module although it is usually best to put it as the first line for easy identification. The PARM statement may also be used more than once in a module to re-assign the parameter values or to assign them to different variables.

If more values are passed into the module than the module picks up, all the values in the PARM statement will be assigned values and the remaining values will be ignored. For example if REPEAT in the example above were called with:

```
REPEAT C$, 2, N, 5
```

the "N" and the "5" would be ignored since REPEAT only has 2 parameters in its PARM statement.

If not enough values are passed into the module, the first variables in the PARM statement will receive values and the remainder will receive no values. For example, if REPEAT is called with:

```
REPEAT "$"
```

then A$ would receive "$", but N would remain 0. If REPEAT were called with no parameters, neither A$ nor N would receive any values. S$ would remain "" (the null string) and N would be 0 (zero).

Parameters may optionally be specified with surrounding square brackets (see USING MODULES). For example:

```
REPEAT ["$",3]
```

PARM also returns a value so it may be used as a function. The value return is the number of parameters passed. This is very useful for modules that have a variable number of parameters. For example, let's create a module MAXIMUM that returns the largest value passed to it:

```
10  N = PARM A(1),A(2),A(3),A(4),A(5),A(6),A(7),
    A(8),A(9),A(10)
20  MAX = 0
30  FOR I = 1 TO N: IF A(I) > MAX THEN MAX = A(I)
40  NEXT
50  EXIT MAX: REM Return largest value
```

MAXIMUM could then be called with any number of values as parameters. In this example only the first 10 would be picked up, though.

```
A = MAX 3,10,7,2      would return 10 to A
```

14

Variable Parameters

Sometimes when a BASIC module is called with parameters, it is desirable to have the module actually change the values of the parameters. These parameters are call variable parameters and are specified by preceding them with an equals sign (=). For example, let's write a module that when called will return the horizontal and vertical positions of the cursor. We will call the module CURSOR.

```
10  PARM X,Y
20  X = PEEK(36):Y = PEEK(37):IF PEEK(49183)
    > 127 THEN X = PEEK(1403): REM The last
    statement is for IIe/IIc 80 columns
30  EXIT
```

If we do:

```
10  A=0:B=0: CURSOR =A, =B
```

then the values of A and B will get passed to X and Y and any values assigned to X and Y in the module CURSOR will change A and B. Since these are variable parameters, the module CURSOR will not create the variables X and Y, but will actually use the variables A and B under assumed the names X and Y. If, when calling CURSOR, we forget to place "=" in front of the variable names, the values for A and B will get passed into the module CURSOR and X and Y will receive those values but any changes to X and Y will not be reflected in A and B.

The following statements are valid:

```
CURSOR =WIDTH, =HEIGHT
TEST =T$, =X%
TEST =T$, =X%
```

but the following are not:

```
CURSOR =2*X, =PEEK(800)      Must be variable name only
CURSOR =I%, =J$              Variable types do not match
```

Note that for variable parameters you must pass a variable name only. You may not pass an expression as a variable parameter. Variable types must also match strictly. Real variables must be passed to real variables (and not to integers), integers to integers (not reals) and strings to strings.

Entire arrays can be passed into a module as variable parameters. Individual elements of an array may be passed as standard parameters but to pass an entire array requires it be used as a variable parameter. Variable array parameters are specified with the "=" and the array name in parenthesis:

```
MODULE =(A), =(S$), =(B1%)
```

The following module, COPY, will copy elements from one array into another:

```
10   PARM A, B, N
20   FOR I = 1 TO N: B(I) = A(I): NEXT : EXIT
```

The following will copy the first 7 elements from array Q to array R:

```
FOR I=1 TO 7: Q(I) = I*I: NEXT
COPY =(Q), =(R), 7
FOR I=1 TO 7: PRINT R(I):NEXT
```

The following function, AMAX, will return the index of the largest element in an integer array:

```
10   PARM A%,N
20   X = A%(1): IDX = 1
30   FOR I = 1 TO N
40   IF A%(I) > X THEN X = A%(I): IDX = I
50   NEXT
60   EXIT IDX
```

and could be called thus:

```
10   MX = AMAX =(AGE%),10
```

Recursion

ProBASIC allows recursion – that is a module may call itself. The following example shows how a module that calculates factorials may use recursion. A factorial of a number is that number times may use recursion. A factorial of a number is that number times every positive number less than itself. For example:

```
FACTORIAL 5 = 5 * 4 * 3 * 2 * 1 = 120
```

Make Factoral

```
10  PARM N: IF N=1THEN 30
20  N = N * FACTORIAL N-1
30  EXIT N
```

If you then call FACTORIAL with a value of 5, it will call itself 5 times before finally returning the value 120 at the first level. Use FLAG 3 to watch how this happens. For a more complete description on recursion it is recommended that you read a good manual on Pascal.

ELSE – for IF/THEN/ELSE statements

Many versions of BASIC have a built-in ELSE statement that allows IF/THEN/ELSE statements but Applesoft does not. With ELSE, if an IF statement is true, everything is executed until the end of the line or until an ELSE statement is hit. If the statement is false, nothing on the line is executed unless the line also contains an ELSE statement in which case everything after the ELSE is executed.

The ELSE statement must appear on the same line as the accompanying IF statement. If a line contains an ELSE and no IF, nothing after the ELSE will be executed.

IF/THEN/ELSE statements may be nested with each ELSE going to the most recent IF statement. Example:

```
10  GET A$
20  IF A$ = "Y" THEN PRINT "YES": ELSE PRINT "NO"
100 IF X = 10 THEN PRINT X: IF Y = 30 THEN
    PRINT Y: ELSE PRINT "Y IS NOT 30"
```

In the above example, the ELSE goes with the most recent IF which is the 2nd one. The first IF has no matching ELSE. In this example, nothing will occur if X does not equal 10.

FLAG flag number [, flag number ...] – Turns on and off
ProBASIC features

FLAG allows you to turn on and off certain features of *ProBASIC*. Specifying a positive value for a flag number turns the feature on while a negative number turns the feature off. The following indicates the flag numbers and their functions:

1: Highlights module names when listing a program by printing them in inverse.

2: Highlights all REM's in a program.

3: Performs module tracing during program execution. It is a very valuable debugging feature. As each BASIC module is called, the calling module's name is printed along with the module being called and the values of all parameters being passed in the following format:

```
/calling module/ -> /called module/ ,value 1,value 2,...
```

If the module is called from the main program, no calling module is specified.

4: Causes a warning to be printed every time 20 lines have been added to or changed in the program. A "SAVE PROGRAM" message will appear to remind you to save the program on disk so you don't make a large number of changes only to have them wiped out by a power failure or computer crash.

5: Causes the name of the module you are editing to be printed when you enter <RETURN> by itself. This flag is on by default.

CHANGES TO PRODOS

New File Types

A few new file types have been added to ProDOS to support the new *ProBASIC* files. The following lists the file type as indicated in a catalog running under *ProBASIC*, the file type as indicated in a catalog without *ProBASIC*, and a brief description of the file.

MOD ($F5) – A BASIC module.

PRG ($F6) – *ProBASIC* program including all modules.

LNK ($F8) – A re-locatable machine language file created by *Merlin Pro* assembler.

The ProDOS command LOAD will load a standard BAS program or a *ProBASIC* PRG program. The SAVE command always saves a program as type PRG. All BASIC and ML modules are saved along with the main program.

Built-In DOS Commands

ProBASIC has two built-in DOS commands for easily loading modules from disk and saving BASIC modules to disk. The format for the commands is:

```
MODLOAD file name
MODSAVE file name
```

The file name is also the module name. For example, this will all load a module called "SORT" from disk and give it the module name "SORT":

```
MODLOAD SORT
MODLOAD /RAM/SORT
MODLOAD /DISK1/SUB3/SORT
MODLOAD SORT,S6,D2
```

21

MODLOAD will load machine language modules of the following types:

REL — Created with Apple's EDASM assembler or others.

LNK — ($F8) created with *Merlin Pro* assembler.

BIN — Make sure it contains no internal absolute addresses (it is re-locatable).

MODLOAD will load BASIC modules of the following types:

MOD — ($F5) created using the MODSAVE command.

BAS — A standard BASIC program used as a subroutine.

MODSAVE saves BASIC modules as type MOD. Since MODLOAD and MODSAVE are DOS commands and not modules, if you want to use them within a program, you will need to use them in the following format as with all DOS commands:

```
PRINT CHR$(4) "MODLOAD TEST"
```

If you load a module with the same name as a BASIC command or function, the module will replace it. For example, if you load a module called PRINT, any statements you add to the program will use the module PRINT instead of the BASIC command PRINT. NOTE: Loading machine language modules causes all the variables to be cleared.

You may save the main program (MAIN) as a module but you may not reload it as the main program. You may, however, rename the MAIN file and load it in as a different BASIC module. The main program can then call it.

For example, if you wish to use the main program from PROGRAM1 in PROGRAM2, use the MODSAVE command to save MAIN from program1. Then, rename the file to something else such as MAIN2. You can then load PROGRAM2 and use MODLOAD to load MAIN2 into PROGRAM2. The main program in PROGRAM 2 can then call MAIN2.

Possible Errors

REQUIRES: module name

If you are using MODLOAD to load a MOD module, the module may call other modules that have not been loaded yet. You will need to load the other module(s) before you can load this module.

DUPLICATE PATH NAME

You are trying to load a module that already exists. You must rename the file if you want to load it in under a different module name.

FILE NOT FOUND

You were either using MODLOAD and the specified file does not exist, or you were using MODSAVE and the module name does not exist.

LIBRARY MODULES

Any module that is saved on disk and can be implemented in any other program is a library module. Several machine language library modules are on the *ProBASIC* disk. A description of each of them follows.

The source code for many of them has been supplied on the disk under the subdirectory SOURCE. They were developed on the *Merlin Pro* assembler but should be compatible with most ProDOS assemblers. Browse through these if you would like to learn how to write your own machine language modules or you may change them to suit your own programming needs.

==

ANYKEY – Stops the program and waits for the user to input any key. No cursor is displayed.

Example: `PRINT "PRESS ANY KEY";: ANYKEY`

==

BUFFER x – Allocates X bytes of memory for the program to use

Returns: Address of start of memory allocated

Often a BASIC program will need some bytes to store some data, set up a parameter list, etc. BUFFER is a function that allocates the number of bytes specified and returns the address of the allocated memory. The buffer is created by moving up the variables of the current module or main program.

If BUFFER is used by a BASIC module, the buffer may be used by any modules the current module calls, but should not be used by any modules that call the current module (the current module should not pass the buffer address back to the calling module).

Example:

```
A = BUFFER 1000          Creates a buffer of 1000 bytes and
                         assigns A the address of the buffer.
```

===

CASE expression, expression GOTO/GOSUB line number [, ...]
— Allows branching to a line number based on the value of a numeric or string expression.

CASE is similar to ON x GOTO/GOSUB but it is much more flexible. String expressions may be used in addition to numeric expressions, numeric values do not need to be consecutive and you may freely mix GOTO's and GOSUB's within the same statement. The first expression is evaluated and a match is searched for in the expressions that follow. If a match is found, a GOTO or GOSUB will occur. If no match is found, program execution will resume at the end of the statement. If a GOSUB occurs, after the RETURN, execution will resume at the end of the statement.

Examples:

```
GET A$: CASE A$,"A" GOTO 100,"B" GOSUB 200,"C"
        GOTO 300:PRINT
```

A$ is compared to each value. If it is "A", a branch will occur to 100. If it is "C" a branch will occur to 300. If it is "B" the subroutine at 200 is called and on RETURN will resume at the PRINT statement. If A$ is not equal to "A", "B", or "C", the PRINT at the end is executed.

```
CASE A*B, 300 GOTO 10, 3*A(I) GOSUB 20, 1/PEEK(24)
GOTO 30
```

==

CLICK – Clicks the speaker

CLICK clicks the speaker just like A = PEEK (49200) but it does it so much faster that high frequency tones can be generated from BASIC.

Example:

```
N = 100: FOR I = 1 TO N: CLICK: NEXT
```

==

DEC numeric variable – Decrements a variable

Returns: Value of decremented variable

DEC is used to decrement the value of a real or integer variable. It is faster than an expression like A = A - 1 and is much faster and clearer than something like ACT%(ID-AGE(IX1)) = ACT%(ID-AGE(IX1)) - 1. DEC may also be used as a function since it returns the value of the decremented variable.

Examples:

`DEC A`	Decrements A.
`DEC ACT%(ID-AGE(IX1))`	Decrements that horrible expression.
`B = DEC A%`	Decrements A% and assigns the decremented.
`B = DEC A%`	Decrements A% and assigns the decremented value to B.
`IF DEC(B) > 0 THEN 100`	Decrements B and if the result is > 0, goes to 100.

27

===

DISK **prefix/module name [, ...]** − Where to load disk-based modules from and/or convert modules into disk-based modules.

A disk-based module is one that must be loaded from disk (including hard disk or RAM disk) each time it is called by the program. By using disk-based modules, a programmer is not limited to the amount of memory normally available for BASIC programs. Part or even most of the program can reside on disk and only occupies main memory when it is actually executing. To determine which modules in the program are disk-based, do a HELP. Each disk-based module will indicate DISK instead of an address. Either BASIC or machine language modules may be disk-based.

To create a machine language disk-based module, use the MODLOAD command to load a machine language program with only 1 byte, then use the DISK command to convert it to a disk-based module.

To create a BASIC disk-based module, create the module with MAKE. If you have not already saved the program lines for the module, type them in and then use the MODSAVE command to save the module to disk. To recover the program space taken up by the module, use DEL to delete all the lines in the module. Then use the DISK command and specify the name of the module as one of the parameters. You may later convert the BASIC module into a non-disk-based module by editing it with EDIT if you desire. You may NOT use the MODLOAD command to reload the module since it already exists.

If you want to use a BASIC module as a disk-based module that you or another programmer has written that already exists on disk, simply create the module with MAKE and use DISK to convert it to a disk-based module. You do not need to use MODLOAD to load it into memory.

Besides converting modules to disk-based modules, the DISK module is used to specify the ProDOS prefix to be used when loading the disk-based modules. The directory may be either a ProDOS volume name or a subdirectory including a "/" at the end.

All disk-based modules will then be loaded from that directory. For maximum speed, it is recommended that the modules be loaded into a RAM disk, but hard disk drives and even floppies will work.

You may change the prefix during program execution to indicate the position of different modules or even different versions of the same module. For example if you have a disk-based module called EVALUATE and you specify the prefix as /DISK1/COWS/ you could later specify /DISK1/PIGS/ or /RAM/ as the prefix and load in a totally different version of EVAULATE with a totally different function. This is a very powerful feature of *ProBASIC* that must be used with the utmost of care. It is normally very dangerous to have the contents of a program change while it is running.

It is recommended that only infrequently-used modules be disk-based such as error-handling modules, sorting modules, printing modules, etc. Otherwise your program may spend most of the computer's time loading modules from disk or /RAM. If your program has a number of different applications which are all called from a main menu, you may decide to have the main menu as a memory-based module or the main program and have each application as disk-based. Frequently used modules that the different applications use may also be memory-based.

Note that a disk-based module does actually take up program space while it is executing and if it calls another disk-based module, you will need to have enough free memory for both of the modules. As soon as you exit a module, the memory is recovered and if the program calls the module again, it must be reloaded.

Examples:

```
DISK "/RAM/"
```
   Load disk-based modules from /RAM.

```
DISK A$, BLUE, RED, GREEN
```
   Specify the prefix according to the value of A$ and convert the BASIC modules BLUE, RED, and GREEN to disk-based.

```
DISK CLOWN
```
   Converts the module CLOWN to disk-based.

===

FACTORIAL x – Returns the factorial of X

The factorial of a number is the product of itself and every integer less than itself. For example, the factorial of 6 is 6*5*4*3*2*1 = 720. The maximum value for X is 33.

Examples:

```
PRINT FACTORIAL 7        Prints 5040.

A = FACTORIAL 33         A gets 8.68331E36.
```

===

HEX integer – Converts decimal to hexadecimal (base 16)

Returns: Hexadecimal value as a string

HEX is a function that returns a string value for the hexadecimal equivalent of the parameter. The string returned starts with a dollar sign ($) and contains exactly 4 hexadecimal digits. The integer parameter must be less than 32768 and greater than or equal to -32768.

Examples:

```
A$ = HEX 124            A$ receives "$007C".

PRINT HEX 256*8         Prints $0800.
```

==

HGR – Fast HGR command
HGR2 – Fast HGR2 command

HGR and HGR2 are library modules that replace their BASIC counterparts. They both clear the screen much faster and do not display the hi-res screen until it has been cleared so you don't have to watch the screen clear itself.

==

INC numeric variable – Increments a variable

Returns: Value of incremented variable

INC is used to increment the value of a real or integer variable. It is similar to the DEC module.

Examples:

See examples under DEC module.

==

LOCATE htab, vtab – Positions the cursor

Use the LOCATE module to specify the position of the cursor in one statement. It replaces the two BASIC statements HTAB and VTAB.

Examples:

```
LOCATE 3,10        The same as doing "HTAB 3: VTAB 10"
LOCATE H,V
```

==

PI – Returns the value of pi (3.14159)

Examples:

```
C = 2*PI*R
PRINT PI*R*R
```

==

REST x – Waits X/10 seconds

Pauses for 1/10 seconds times the value of the parameter.

Examples:

```
REST 25              Waits 2.5 seconds.
REST S * 10          Waits S seconds.
```

==

ROUND numeric expression – Rounds a number

Returns: Rounded value of the numeric expression

ROUND is like INT except that if the fractional portion is greater or equal to .5, rounding up occurs.

Examples:

```
A = INT (3.1)        Returns 3
A = ROUND 3.1        Returns 3

A = INT (7.7)        Returns 7
A = ROUND 7.7        Returns 8
```

===

VARS – Does a variable dump

VARS lists the names and values of all the simple variables that the BASIC program has created. Note that there are no variables until a program has run and only those variables that have been assigned values are actually created. VARS does not list the arrays.

===

VIRTUAL [file name [, array (size) [LEN string length] [, ...]]]
– Provides for use of disk-based arrays of nearly unlimited size

Normally arrays reside in memory and must share memory with the program and any other variables. With VIRTUAL, a ProDOS file is created within which the arrays reside and they do not take up even 1 byte of main memory. Furthermore, the arrays don't even take up any space in the ProDOS file unless you actually assign values to the arrays. Since the arrays reside in a file but are used exactly the same way normal arrays are used, it is as though you virtually have a lot more memory.

The size of the arrays is only limited by the size of the ProDOS device that will contain the arrays. A standard floppy disk will hold about five times as much array information as is normally available. Standard /RAM gives over two times as much and some of the memory extension cards can raise that up to as much as 50 times as much array space. For unusually large arrays, it may be necessary to use a hard disk.

The use of floppy disks with VIRTUAL is discouraged because of the extreme degradation in program speed. Each time a value is assigned to an element of an array or anytime an element of an array is used in an expression, a disk access must be made.

Virtual arrays are used the same way that normal arrays are used. The only change needed is to add the VIRTUAL statement itself. The first parameter for VIRTUAL is the name of the ProDOS file that will contain the arrays.

The parameters following are the names of the arrays that will reside in the file. These are declared exactly the same as with a DIM statement with one exception. For string arrays, it is necessary to dimension a maximum length for each string in the array. With virtual arrays, each element of a string array takes up the maximum size for each element even if the value assigned to that element is only one character long. If, for example, you dimension "A$" as a virtual array with maximum length 100 and you do $A\$(5) = $ "I", the single character "I" will take up 100 bytes of disk space. If you do not specify a string length, the default is 40. The maximum is 254. Make the string length as small as possible but if you ever attempt to assign a string to the array that is longer than the maximum length, you will get a "STRING TOO LONG" error.

A maximum of 20 arrays may be declared in a VIRTUAL statement and each array may have a maximum of four dimensions and each dimension has a maximum index of 32768.

If the file already exists when you do a VIRTUAL statement and at least one array is specified, the file will be deleted before it is created again and any array information in the file is lost. If no arrays are specified, then the file is opened for virtual array use and it is not deleted first. This means that the arrays were actually stored on disk for reuse. One program may create the array file and another may use the values in the arrays. Note that the programmer will have to remember which arrays are in the file since the 2nd program that uses the arrays does not specify in its virtual statement the names of the arrays.

A VIRTUAL statement with no parameters should always be used at the end of a program to make sure the file is properly closed. Editing the program, RUNning the program, or loading another program will close the file, but it is still a good idea always to use a VIRTUAL statement at the end of a program that uses virtual arrays. Files left open can cause problems for ProDOS.

More than one VIRTUAL statement can be used in a program but only 1 file may be open at a time. Each time a VIRTUAL statement is used, any open virtual array file is closed and a new one may be opened with the same or different arrays.

IMPORTANT: VIRTUAL should not be used as a disk-based module. It must remain in memory.

Examples:

```
VIRTUAL "/RAM/ARRAYS", A(10000), B%(3000,100),
        S$(1000) LEN 10, C$(100), D(10,10,10,10)
```

> The arrays A,B%,S$,C$, and D will reside in the file /RAM/ ARRAYS. The strings in S$ have a maximum length of 10 characters. The strings in C$ have the default maximum length of 40 characters.

```
VIRTUAL "/BUSINESS/DATA"
```

> Will open the file /BUSINESS/DATA that already exists and use the arrays in it as virtual arrays.

```
VIRTUAL
```

> Will close an open virtual array file.

ADDITIONAL LIBRARIES

These additional machine language module libraries were published by The Software Touch.

```
================================
```
LIBRARY 1 – by Rob Renstrom
```
================================
```

DEC   Converts hexadecimal to decimal.

INKEY   Returns the current key that is pressed without stopping as GET does.

INSTR   Searches a string for the location of a substring and returns its position.

LINE INPUT   Allows you to enter strings containing commas and colons without the ?EXTRA IGNORED error message.

REPT   Repeat any string, X number of times.

SCREEN   Clears or inverses any portion of the text screen.

SORT   High-speed array sorter. Sorts single DIM string, integer, or real arrays with optional "tag" array. Allows optional starting and ending array elements for all arrays and starting and ending character positions for string arrays. Sample sort times for string arrays: 2.60 seconds for 500 elements; 6.38 seconds for 1000; and 14.4 seconds for 2000.

TONE   Tone generator. Used to create all kinds of sounds.

============================

LIBRARY 2 — by Alan Bird

============================

BUTTON x — Determines the status of the paddle buttons or Open-Apple and Solid-Apple keys

Returns: VTRUE (1) if button X (0 or 1) is pressed or FALSE (0) if the button is not pressed.

Example:

```
10  IF BUTTON 0 THEN PRINT "BUTTON 0 IS PRESSED."
20  IF BUTTON 1 THEN PRINT "BUTTON 1 IS PRESSED."
```

==

CIRCLE x,y,radius [,ratio] — Draw hi-res circles and ellipses

CIRCLE draws a circle on the hi-res graphics screen with its center at X,Y and a radius of length RADIUS. RATIO is an optional parameter used for drawing ellipses. It indicates the ratio of the radius on the Y-axis compared to the radius on the X-axis. The x-axis radius is equal to RADIUS while the Y-axis radius is equal to RATIO * RADIUS.

Circle does automatic clipping so if a portion of the circle will not fit on the screen, it does not produce an error or wrap-around but simply does not draw that portion of the circle.

Example:

```
10  HGR: HCOLOR = 3
20  FOR I = 1 TO 3
30  CIRCLE 100,100,50,I
40  NEXT
```

==

CONV decimal number/hexadecimal number – Conversions

      CONV displays the decimal and hexadecimal equivalents of a decimal or hexadecimal number.

Examples:

`CONV 100`	Prints "100 $0064".
`CONV $80`	Prints "128 $0080".

==

DATE [string] – Sets and reads the ProDOS date

      DATE sets the ProDOS date. The date is used by ProDOS when saving or create files and is used by other programs for printing reports, etc.

      The parameter is a string in this format: "DAY-MONTH-YEAR" where month is the 3-character abbreviation for the month. DAY is 1 or 2 digits and year is 2 digits.

      DATE also returns the value of the assigned date. If no parameter is supplied, it does not set the date but only reads it.

Examples:

`DATE "1-AUG-85"`	Sets date to August 1, 1985.
`A$ = DATE "31-JUL-62"`	Sets date to July 31, 1962 and returns that date in A$.
`PRINT DATE`	Prints whatever the current date happens to be set to.

40

==

DELETE string, index, count — Deletes a substring from a string

DELETE deletes a substring from the STRING parameter starting from INDEX and deleting COUNT characters.

Example:

```
10  A$ = "THE SOFTWARE TOUCH"
20  DELETE A$,5,9
30  PRINT A$                    Prints "THE TOUCH"
```

==

ERASE array [, ...] — Deletes an array from memory

Often an array is DIM'ed and used for some purpose and never used again. It is, however, taking up memory space which may eventually lead to an "OUT OF MEMORY" error. With ERASE, when you are finished with an array, you can delete it. If for some reason you need the array again, you can re-DIM it.

NOTE: This module can't be used when using the **VIRTUAL** module.

Example:

```
ERASE A, B%, C$      Deletes arrays A, B%, and C$ which may
                     have been dimensioned thus:
                     DIM A(200,3), B%(1000), C$(5)
```

41

==

ERROR **number** – Generates the indicated error

     ERROR is used to generate an error for testing ONERR GOTO's, indicating after a RESUME what the error was, fooling your friends, etc. The following tables indicate the appropriate error numbers to generate the indicated errors.

ProDOS errors:

```
  2:Range Error
  3:No Device Connected
  4:Write Protected
  5:End of Data
6,7:Path Not Found
  8:I/O Error
  9:Disk Full
 10:File Locked
 11:Invalid Parameter
 12:No Buffers Available
 13:File Type Mismatch
 14:Program Too Large
 15:Not Direct Command
 17:Directory Full
 18:File Not Open
 19:Duplicate File Name
 20:File Busy
 21:File(s) Still Open
```

BASIC errors:

```
  0:Next Without FOR
 16:Syntax Error
 22:RETURN without GOSUB
 42:Out of Data
 53:Illegal Quantity
 69:Overflow
 77:Out of Memory
 90:Undef'd Statement
107:Bad Subscript
120:Redim'd Array
133:Division by Zero
163:Type Mismatch
176:String Too Long
191:Formula Too Complex
224:Undef'd Function
```


Example:

ERROR 16   Causes a SYNTAX error.

42

==

FILLCHAR address, count, byte value —
Fills a range of memory with the specified byte value

Use FILLCHAR to quickly fill a range of memory with a certain byte value.

Example:

```
FILLCHAR 8192,8192,0      Quickly blanks out Hi-res Screen 1.
```

==

FORINT — FOR statement that uses an integer variable

Use FORINT if you are using an integer variable to index with. You must use this with NEXTINT! Do not attempt to use FORINT with NEXT!

A FOR/NEXT loop that uses FORINT is much faster than the standard FOR if you do not use the integer variable for any reason. Integer variables require more time to evaluate than do floating point variables.

Example:

```
10  FORINT I% = 1 TO 1000
20  CLICK
30  NEXTINT
```

43

===

INSERT substring, string, index – Inserts a substring into a
string

INSERT is used to insert SUBSTRING into STRING at the position INDEX.

Example:

```
10  A$ = "THE TOUCH"
20  INSERT "SOFTWARE ",A$,5
30  PRINT A$            Prints "THE SOFTWARE TOUCH"
```

===

LAND integer, integer – Performs a logical AND of the
2 parameters

LAND does a 2-byte bit-by-bit AND of the 2 parameters and returns the result. Only the bits set in both the 1st parameter and the 2nd parameter will be set. Used for testing bits.

Example:

```
IF LAND PEEK(49152),128 THEN 100
```

If the high bit of 49152 is set (a key has been pressed), go to 100.

```
X = LAND Y,Z
```

AND Y and Z and assign to X.

==

LINEFIND line number – Finds a BASIC line

LINEFIND returns the address of the BASIC line number. If the line does not exist, 0 is returned.

Example:

```
A = LINEFIND 150
```
The address of line 150 is returned in A.

==

LOR integer, integer – Performs a logical OR of the 2 parameters

LOR does a 2-byte bit-by-bit OR of the 2 parameters and returns the result. Any bit that is set in the 1st parameter or in the 2nd parameter will be set in the result. Used for setting bits.

Example:

```
X = LOR X,32
```
Set bit 5 in X.

==

MOD dividend/divisor – Returns the remainder from division

MOD is a function that used to be in Integer BASIC but does not appear in Applesoft BASIC. It is used to determine the remainder from division. Most often it is used in calculating byte values.

Examples:

```
A = MOD 100,3
```
A = 1 because 100/3 has a remainder of 1

```
10  LO = MOD A,256
20  HI = INT(A/256)
```
Calculate high and low bytes of a 2-byte value.

==

NEXTINT – See FORINT

==

PAGE – Outputs a form feed character (Control-L)

Example:

```
10  PRINT CHR$(4)"PR#1"
20  PRINT "NEXT PAGE"
30  PAGE
```
Goes to the next page.

==

PPEEK address – Two byte PEEK

Returns the 2-byte value at the specified address.

Example:

The expression: `A = PPEEK 54`
Is equivalent to: `A = PEEK(54) + 256 * PEEK(55)`

==

PPOKE address, value – Two byte POKE

POKE's a 2-byte value into memory.

Example:

`PPOKE 54,8192`   Redirects output to $2000.

==

READBLOCK slot, drive, block, [address] –
Reads a block from a ProDOS disk or other device

READBLOCK reads one block (512) bytes from any ProDOS device (floppy disk, hard disk, RAM disk, etc). You must specify the SLOT and DRIVE parameters for the device as well as the BLOCK to be read. If you do not specify the ADDRESS parameter, the block will be read into the temporary 1K buffer just above HIMEM.

Example:

`READBLOCK 3,2,2`   Reads in the 1st block of the volume directory in /RAM.

47

==

RESTORE [line number] – Restore DATA to a specific line number

This module replaces the BASIC RESTORE command and allows you to optionally RESTORE to a specified line number, therefore adding selectivity in using the READ statement.

Example:

```
10  RESTORE 40
20  READ A$              Will read "BANANA" instead of "APPLE"
30  DATA APPLE
40  DATA BANANA
```

==

RESUME [line number]/[NEXT] – Resume after an ONERR to a specific line number or to the next statement

The RESUME module without any parameters behaves the same as the BASIC RESUME command. With a line number specified, it will RESUME to the specified line number instead of back to the statement that caused the error. With the "NEXT" parameter, it will resume with the statement after the one that caused the error.

Examples:

```
10  ONERR GOTO 100
20  PRINT "INSERT DISK AND PRESS RETURN": GET A$
30  PRINT CHR$(4)"OPEN FILE"
...
100 PRINT "CAN'T OPEN FILE!":RESUME 20: REM BACK TO
    "INSERT DISK ..."

10  ONERR GOTO 100
20  PRINT CHR$(4)"CATALOG":PRINT "ANY KEY":GET A$
...
100  PRINT "CAN'T CATALOG": RESUME NEXT: REM GOES BACK
    TO "ANY KEY", DON'T CATALOG AGAIN
```

48

==

STACK – Displays the contents of the system stack

STACK is a module that is useful for learning how BASIC uses the system stack (at $100) and can also be used in debugging machine language modules that need to leave information on the stack. STACK lists the address and contents in hexadecimal of the stack from the current stack pointer to the very top of the stack ($1FF). FOR and GOSUB both leave information on the stack:

FOR leaves 18 bytes:

2 - TXTPTR (address in BASIC program of statement following FOR
2 - CURLIN (line number of next statement)
5 - Final value for variable index (in floating point format)
1 - Sign of STEP value
5 - STEP value (in floating point format)
2 - Address of index variable
1 - FOR token ($81)

GOSUB leaves 7 bytes:

2 - Return address ($D7D2)
2 - TXTPTR (address in BASIC program to RETURN to)
2 - CURLIN (line number to RETURN to)
1 - GOSUB token ($B0)

Example:

```
10   STACK
20   FOR I = 1 TO 5
30   PRINT I
40   STACK
50   NEXT
```

===

TIME [string] – Sets and reads the ProDOS time

      TIME sets the ProDOS time. The time is used by ProDOS when saving or create files and is used by other programs for printing reports, etc. The parameter is a string in this format: "HOUR:MINUTE" where HOUR is 1 or 2 digits and MINUTE is 2 digits. TIME also returns the value of the ProDOS time. If no parameter is supplied, it does not set the time but only reads it.

Examples:

```
TIME "4:05"
```
Sets the time to 4:05.

```
A$ = TIME "16:07"
```
Sets the time to 16:07 (4:07 pm) and returns that time in A$.

```
PRINT TIME
```
Prints whatever the current time happens to be set to.

===

UPPER string variable – Converts a string to upper case

      UPPER converts a string to upper case. This may be necessary if your program may run on an Apple II or II Plus that does not have lowercase capability.

Example:

```
10  IIE = (PEEK(64435) = 6): REM True if IIe or IIc
20  A$ = "Welcome to this program"
30  IF NOT IIE THEN UPPER A$: REM If not IIe or
    IIc, convert to upper case
40  PRINT A$
```

==

VARPTR variable – Finds a variable

     VARPTR returns the address of the BASIC variable. If the variable does not already exist, it will be created. The address of an element of an array may be found also.

Examples:

A = VARPTR C$ The address of C$ is returned in A.

A = VARPTR D%(5)   The address of the 5th element of D% is
                       returned in A.

==

WINDOW htab, vtab, width, height, text –
Displays text in an inverse window on screen

     WINDOW will display text in a variable-size window anywhere on a 40-column or 80-column (IIe or IIc only) screen. It also saves the information under the window so it can be restored. The text is displayed in inverse with an inverse border.

     The HTAB and VTAB parameters indicate the position of the window on the screen. The WIDTH and HEIGHT parameters indicate the width and height of the entire window. The area for the text inside the window will actually be 2 characters smaller for width and height since there is a border around the window.

     A '/' character implies a <RETURN> and causes the text to go to the next line. WINDOW will not automatically break text between words so you will need to use the '/' to do proper formatting without splitting lines in the middle of the words.

     WINDOW without any parameters will restore the text that was on the screen before the last WINDOW command.

51

Example:

```
...
100  WINDOW 10,10,18,8,"THIS IS AN/EXAMPLE OF HOW/
     THE WINDOW/MODULE CAN SHOW/INFORMATION ON/THE
     SCREEN."
110  GET A$: WINDOW: REM Restores screen
```

==

WRITEBLOCK slot, drive, block, [address] –
Writes a block to a ProDOS disk or other device

WRITEBLOCK writes one block (512) bytes to any ProDOS device (floppy disk, hard disk, RAM disk, etc). You must specify the SLOT and DRIVE parameters for the device as well as the BLOCK to be written. If you do not specify the ADDRESS parameter, the block will be written from the temporary 1K buffer just above HIMEM.

WARNING! This is an extremely dangerous module and must be used with the utmost of care. Never use it to write to any disk that has not been backed up!

Example:

```
WRITEBLOCK 6,1,2        Writes to the 1st block of the volume
                        directory on the disk in Slot 6 Drive 1.
```

==

XOR integer, integer – Performs a logical exclusive-OR of
the 2 parameters

XOR does a 2-byte bit-by-bit XOR of the 2 parameters and returns the result. Exclusive-OR sets any bit in the result that is in one parameter or the other but no in both.

```
Example:   X = XOR X,Z
```

52

www.ingramcontent.com/pod-product-compliance
Lightning Source LLC
Chambersburg PA
CBHW051214050326
40689CB00008B/1304